The Praying Mommy

THE
PRAYING MOMMY

A 31 Day Devotional

Elrich Martin

The opinions expressed by the author are not necessarily those of Revival Waves of Glory Books & Publishing.

Published by Revival Waves of Glory Books & Publishing

PO Box 596| Litchfield, Illinois 62056 USA

www.revivalwavesofgloryministries.com

Revival Waves of Glory Books & Publishing is committed to excellence in the publishing industry.

Published in the United States of America

ISBN 978-1-68411-174-9

Contents

INTRODUCTION

Hi mommies! This is your answer to peace within the uncertainty of early motherhood, where you do not know what to do as you look at the clock in the early hours of the morning, wishing for your little one to fall asleep so you can also hit the pillow. As I have learned from my wife from her sleepless nights, she has totally placed her faith of the unknown with our baby in the Lord's hands. God knows your frustration, your desires, your needs and your wants. God watches you while you are putting your own needs aside to look and care for your baby as only a mother can. Please read the devotional day by day, reading the scriptures from the Bible to refresh your mind as you take on the uncertainty of the night but with the presence of God by your side. You also have the option to share your thoughts and to share your desires and your progress as you take the day and night on with the Lord by your side. You are blessed and highly favored.

THE TEST WITHIN THE JOY

The day you and your husband have been waiting for, a quick check and two stripes show, the symbol of life and joy, you're pregnant! This is the time when you visualize your baby, a speck at this point already out of the womb and the first kiss you will give your bundle of joy. During these months of waiting for the little one to arrive, you tend to begin to form an unbreakable bond with your little one, as he or she from a tadpole like shape, progresses into a formed human being. The excitement for hubby as Braxton hicks (false labor pains) fuels the anticipation of another addition to the family knocking on the door of the world. You, once very confident at the prospect of delivery, seem more anxious as the time draws closer. The contractions starting as time grows nearer, the pain of new life drawing closer after one final scream in the delivery room, attracts a silence and then a cry of new life. The umbilical cord is cut and that disconnects the life you gave to your little one from the womb and the journey into the world begins. Your husband and family are overjoyed and as sweat drips from your brow and hair, it's a testimony of a battle won. You sigh of relief as the long awaited trial is over and looking in your newborn baby's eyes is all worth the effort. Thinking, by yourself of the baby fat you will be losing and the things you can now do and eat that you could not during this nine months period of sacrifice. It's all over, you think, but is it? From day one, most babies suffer from colic which leaves mommies with sleepless nights, red eyes, feeling hopeless at times and not the once confident woman as you once were. As with a lion which were caught and placed in captivity, at first you will see the determination in its eyes when it has all intentions to overcome this obstacle but as the days, weeks and months pass, you will notice that the shine in that once fearless lions eyes will start to fade away as the light of faith grows dimmer and dimmer. One would think that I can relate to what you are facing. Well, yes and no. I'm a man but I'm also a husband and have been giving an exclusive report on how mommies feel from one expert, my wife. This is our second child. With our first child it was smooth sailing with her sleeping during the night and being awake during the day which was heaven to us but our second child brought us back to earth to the reality faced by millions of mommies around the world, from all different lifestyles, backgrounds, races or religion. This is the one thing most all woman can relate with and share their experiences very similar in occurrence - meaning sleepless nights and crying little ones with most times no relief. Drops or ointments may bring a little relief but the reality for most is that it will be outgrown by most babies. Being awake for two hours in one night might not be so bad if it's the first nights experience of colic but as the days go on and the hours of lack of sleep increases, it is even clear for a man to understand what it can do to one's state of mind. The average person sleeps eight hours a day, which for a week can be plus or minus fifty-six hours per week but if you only get two or three hours sleep as day, it can test even the toughest individual. I can never relate to the strength for a mother during that phase as a new mother or a mother of five and the tests you go through which shows the strength a woman possesses and the gift they have but there is an answer for all the tests in our lives and how we deal with what is not the natural and causing us to feel as if our lives have taken a turn for the worst. I hope the 31 days of encouragement will be an inspiration for all woman during this period and as they read the scriptures day by day, that they will feel inspired to press on and that in faith the hours of sleep for them and baby will become more and lack of sleep will diminish and that God's word will be their lullaby in faith and an answer to their prayers.

DAY ONE

Proverbs 31:25-30

"Strength and dignity are her clothing, and she laughs at the time to come. She opens her mouth with wisdom, and the teaching of kindness is on her tongue. She looks well to the ways of her household and does not eat the bread of idleness. Her children rise up and call her blessed; her husband also, and he praises her: "Many women have done excellently, but you surpass them all." Charm is deceitful, and beauty is vain, but a woman who fears the Lord is to be praised"

This is the words of God for you during this testing time, mommy. God knows your fears and will keep you during this uncertainty for dealing with the test of looking after a newborn. As it says in the verse, strength and dignity are in her clothing meaning you are a conqueror before this test even started. Make yourself a cup of tea and as you hold your crying baby, confess these words, this test will not last; the storm is over before it started. It is in the strength of character of a woman that her grace lies. She looks well to the ways of her household and does not eat bread of idleness is a confession of your strength that you as a woman have dealing day by

1

day with more and overcoming all that were laid on you is a testimony of your character. God would not have given you this little one if he did not know your ability to stand strong in adversity. Know that you were made as a child of God and a mother to a living being once given to a woman who bore a son that saved the world, named Jesus and mother named Mary. Keep confessing your blessed and highly favored and as the hours pass, pray to God and thank him for the opportunity that he have given you above so many more that wished that they had the opportunity to hold their little one but have not been as fortunate as you. You are chosen and a fearless woman that can overcome everything and meditating on the word through scripture will give you the energy to make it through this night. As you hold your little one, just close your eyes and in faith, visualize him or her sleeping peacefully and it will come to pass because faith is the evidence of things not yet seen but yet believing through the spiritual eye. Feel the time passing more quickly as you visualize your peace within the storm and it might even calm your little one. Letting them lay on your chest will in most cases calm them as they will feel your calm heartbeat which will put them at ease. You are the only one they want near them now; you are their heartbeat, their comfort and so are our lord Jesus Christ. See yourself resting your head on Jesus chest and feel the peace of the holy spirit calming your fears and his everlasting peaceful heartbeat becoming one with yours as you hear him say, be at peace my child, all is well, all is well. You can laugh at the days to come because you are a woman of worth and faith. Confess these words and the night will become less of a burden and more of a victory, Amen.

Prayer for today:

Lord, please order my steps today as I go through this unknown night. Please give me the wisdom to lead through the storm and to be a source of strength through you. In Jesus name, Amen.

Share your thoughts

First night:

How do you feel?

....
....
....
....
....
....
....
....
....
....

What has the word of God taught you?

....
....
....
....
....
....
....

Elrich Martin

....
....
....
....
....
....
....

How are yours and your baby' sleeping hours?

....
....
....
....
....
....
....
....
....
....
....

Is there any improvement and what have you learned?

....
....
....
....
....
....
....
....

The Praying Mommy

....
....
....
....
....
....

DAY TWO

Proverbs 31:26-27

"She opens her mouth with wisdom, and the teaching of kindness is on her tongue. She looks well to the ways of her household and does not eat the bread of idleness."

You are a born leader and a teacher as a woman of God. Every day you lead your family into the daily battle and every day you prepare through wisdom and Gods guidance. Do not forget who you are. You are more than a victim, you are a victor! You have the blood of a king running through you veins as you take on challenges of daily life of words of wisdom and calmness. Read psalm 91 as this will truly give you the strength in any weakness you may feel. I've taken the liberty to add the psalm from the bible and as you read it, confess your fears and God will hear your heart's desire.

Psalm 91

1. Whoever dwells in the shelter of the Most High will rest in the shadow of the Almighty.
2. I will say of the Lord, "He is my refuge and my fortress, my God, in whom I trust."

3. Surely he will save you from the fowler's snare and from the deadly pestilence.
4. He will cover you with his feathers, and under his wings you will find refuge; his faithfulness will be your shield and rampart.
5. You will not fear the terror of night, nor the arrow that flies by day,
6. nor the pestilence that stalks in the darkness, nor the plague that destroys at midday.
7. A thousand may fall at your side, ten thousand at your right hand, but it will not come near you.
8. You will only observe with your eyes and see the punishment of the wicked.
9. If you say, "The Lord is my refuge," and you make the Most High your dwelling,
10. no harm will overtake you; no disaster will come near your tent.
11. For he will command his angels concerning you to guard you in all your ways;
12. they will lift you up in their hands, so that you will not strike your foot against a stone.
13. You will tread on the lion and the cobra; you will trample the great lion and the serpent.
14. "Because he[b] loves me," says the Lord, "I will rescue him; I will protect him, for he acknowledges my name.
15. He will call on me, and I will answer him; I will be with him in trouble, I will deliver him and honor him.
16. With long life I will satisfy him and show him my salvation."

Prayer for today:

Lord, I ask you to guard over my words and for me to speak words of victory and not defeat in all I do. I ask in Jesus name, Amen.

<u>Share your thoughts</u>

Second night:

How do you feel?

....
....
....
....
....
....
....
....
....
....
....

What has the word of God taught you?

....
....
....
....
....
....
....

....
....
....
....

How are yours and your baby's sleeping hours?

....
....
....
....
....
....
....
....
....
....
....

Is there any improvement and what have you learned?

....
....
....
....
....
....
....
....
....
....

Elrich Martin

....
....
....
....

DAY THREE

Isaiah 49:15

"Can a woman forget her nursing child, that she should have no compassion on the son of her womb? Even these may forget, yet I will not forget you."

God thinks so highly of you as a mother that he compares his love for his people to a mother have towards her suckling baby. Is that not so amazing how God sees you as an example of his love for mankind? God is actually saying that maternal love is far more in greatness and above any kind of love and none can compare to you, motherly love. So mothers, woman, wives, single mothers please see yourself as God sees you. He holds you in such high regard for the duty you have as a bearer and a career of life that one cannot comprehend how important you are. Even though you might feel down, in need of a hair transformation and a loss of baby weight and feeling the strain is holding you down, God sees you as his right-hand in raising his sons and daughters into this world.

Your little one has probably fallen asleep on your chest and as you also feel the tiredness coming over, please feel at peace that you are one step closer to the victory and peace is around the corner waiting for you, just hold on.

Prayer for today:

Lord, thank you for your guidance and love, thank you for your hand of grace with us and please give the strength of a mother, in Jesus name I ask, Amen.

Share your thoughts

Third night:

How do you feel?

....
....
....
....
....
....
....
....
....
....
....

What has the word of God taught you?

....
....
....

....
....
....
....
....
....
....
....
....

How are yours and your baby's sleeping hours?

....
....
....
....
....
....
....
....
....
....
....
....

Is there any improvement and what have you learned?

....
....

Elrich Martin

....
....
....
....
....
....
....
....
....
....
....
....

DAY FOUR

Isaiah 66:13

"As one whom his mother comforts, so I will comfort you; you shall be comforted in Jerusalem."

God once an again make reverence to mothers and how your comfort is reflected on Gods beloved Jerusalem. Think about how great it will be one day when you see God and he takes your hand and look into your eyes and say,(your name) and hold you against your chest and say, feel how you made my sons and daughters feel in their newborn form and the comfort you gave them when they needed you most. I congratulate you on being a mother of worth and holding on through the storm. Just imagine how that would feel. I can even visualize that happening to every woman as you truly have Gods maternal love flowing through you. I believe day four is become better and the night is more sleep, even by and hour extra as God is stroking your baby to sleep to allow you to get closer to your hearts cry. By now you might feel that it must just stop now and you wish that a fairy would come and give you three wishes and poof, everything is perfect. Well, that won't happen but the best part is that your faith will bring reality forth and even as if the working of a myth faith, our God of the supernatural is working and moving you closer and closer. Now take a sip of that chamomile tea and read Isaiah 66 and meditate on the world which is your strength.

Prayer for today:

Lord, I know you love me and I know this storm will not last. I thank you for the end of the trial and the beginning of my victory. I ask this all in Jesus name, Amen.

Share your thoughts

Fourth night:

How do you feel?

....
....
....
....
....
....
....
....
....
....
....
....

What has the word of God taught you?

....
....
....
....
....
....
....
....
....
....
....
....

How are yours and your baby's sleeping hours?

....
....
....
....
....
....
....
....
....
....
....
....
....
....

Elrich Martin

Is there any improvement and what have you
learned?

....
....
....
....
....
....
....
....
....
....
....
....
....

DAY FIVE

Proverbs 31:28

"Her children rise up and call her blessed; her husband also, and he praises her."

The day might feel long as you enter the night but you are almost there and have peace in the scripture bas it outlines the importance you have for your household as a trusted wife, a loving mother, a spouse of integrity and a vision of perfection to your Lord Jesus. As you husband sees you so does God see you and those who have accepted Jesus as their spiritual husband. Your little angle cannot express his or her appreciation for you yet as its not yet possible in expression but see the look in their little eyes when you come with the prepared milk bottle to quench their hunger and thirst and when you speak to them even if they can't speak back, but you can sense the love as they look at you. They, at that stage see you as God sees you, a perfection of uniqueness and as they grow older, your affection and love will give them the grace to care for their little ones in their own families one day. Hubby also appreciates you even though some will not say it, they do, trust me. Deep within, most of them, even how stubborn admire you for who you are and how you take care of them and their children. Take heart that the above also refers to God as your spiritual husband who praises you for your works on earth and your tireless approach to you devotion to your duties as a mother, a wife, a friend, a leader, a home executive and a righteous woman of God.

Prayer for today:

Lord, thank you for the privilege of allowing me to be a mother and to fulfill the duties according to your will and guidance. I praise your name, Amen.

Share your thoughts

Fifth night:

How do you feel?

....
....
....
....
....
....
....
....
....
....
....
....

What has the word of God taught you?

....
....
....
....
....
....
....
....
....
....
....
....

How are yours and your baby's sleeping hours?

....
....
....
....
....
....
....
....
....
....
....
....
....
....

Elrich Martin

Is there any improvement and what have you
learned?

....
....
....
....
....
....
....
....
....
....
....
....

DAY SIX

Psalm 113:9

"He gives the barren woman a home, making her the joyous mother of children. Praise the Lord!"

You might at this stage feel a bit more at ease as you are starting to understand the plan God have for you as a mother and that your efforts are not unseen. You might also be a woman who has prayed for years for God to make your womb fruitful and bring forth the life you craved for so long to grow within you. Also if you are a woman who have prayed and at an advance age were given the opportunity to be a mother for the first time, be of good cheer and praise the lord. Where two or more agree, God say in his word that it will be done and I believe you that your dormant womb will be activated with the Holy Spirit and the seed within you will bear fruit. So many women yearn for that cry of the day or night, so many silent tears, waiting for the nine months to start. So many mommies wait for your little ones to arrive and to be at one with them. Rest assured, faith is the evidence of things not yet seen but as you wait for the time to arrive, rub over you womb as though the life within is feeling you touch as God prepares your little one to enter within. Don't stop praising God and expecting and it will be so. The story of Ruth is a testimony for all that it is never too late. Mothers, let this be a word of encouragement of that the privilege you have as vessel of life through God. Be of good cheer that you have been chosen as your little ones guardian as the duty could have gone to anyone else but you were especially chosen for the role. As you meditate on the word of God, be happy as your rest is coming, declare and it will be so. You are at rest, you are at peace, and you are a fearless woman.

Prayer for today:

Thank you, God for opening my womb nine months ago to be able to bring forth my beautiful child. Please forgive me for my doubts and my fears. I trust in you always, Amen.

Share your thoughts

Sixth night:

How do you feel?

....
....
....
....
....
....
....

....
....
....
....
....

What has the word of God taught you?

....
....
....
....
....
....
....
....
....
....
....
....
....
....

How are yours and your baby's sleeping hours?

....
....
....
....
....
....
....

Elrich Martin

....
....
....
....
....
....
....

Is there any improvement and what have you learned?

....
....
....
....
....
....
....
....
....
....
....
....
....

DAY SEVEN

Proverbs 31:31

"Give her of the fruit of her hands, and let her works praise her in the gates."

A good woman is hard to find and is more worth than the rarest of diamonds. Don't underestimate your worth. Your works on earth are being praised in heaven. God have prepared you all the life for the duty as a mother and you are the perfect candidate for the job at hand which cannot be done by everyone, only a select few, namely the female gender. I cannot image what a man would have done in such a situation and the woman say, Amen. I can visualize a man, holding the baby during the night shift, soiled nappies laying everywhere, the milk bottle is empty, no time to fill a fresh one. The place looking a mess as there is no time to clean the house and the other children in the house having to prepare for school themselves and everything is upside down. Can you imagine that? Can you now understand your worth? The fruits of your hands, woman is evident in your ability to keep your household together and being the glue that keeps everything together. Your works are not unseen. God trust you so much that he is leaving a fragile little one in your care. You are being honored in heaven through your nightshift and admired by the angels for your ability to hold on through all storms as only a woman of worth can. Now lift your hands and praise God and thank him for your duty, one that only you can do.

Prayer for today:

Lord, today I stand in front of you as a grateful mother and I'm thankful for all the blessing you give us. Give me the strength to look after my child as you look after us. In Jesus name I ask, Amen.

Share your thoughts

Seventh night:

How do you feel?

....
....
....
....
....
....
....
....
....
....
....
....
....

What has the word of God taught you?

....
....
....
....
....
....
....
....
....
....
....
....

How are yours and your baby's sleeping hours?

....
....
....
....
....
....
....
....
....
....
....
....
....
....

Elrich Martin

Is there any improvement and what have you
learned?

....
....
....
....
....
....
....
....
....
....
....
....
....
....

DAY EIGHT

Proverbs 31:14-16

"She is like the ships of the merchant; she brings her food from afar. She rises while it is yet night and provides food for her household and portions for her maidens. She considers a field and buys it; with the fruit of her hands she plants a vineyard."

Looking at the above verse, it demonstrates the value of your works and the extent of your duties and the quality and quantity thereof. You are a provider to your little one and your household and make the nightly sacrifice for your family. You are defined as bringing food to your household and portions for your maidens. I can define it as how a mother looks after her family, feeding them both with substance and spirit through the word of God and even looking after her neighbors and friends. You have made your household, your field of choice and have chosen to plant your love for the vineyard to grow. Yes, your little one upbringing is the fruit of your hands you will bear the grapes that will grow through your investment in your field of family. Tell yourself, you are a merchant of loaves and you can make it through this time. Declare your worth today. You are blessed and highly favored, woman of God.

Prayer for today:

Lord, I'm tired but I am not weary of your word. I know you have a better plan for me and you will take me through the storm. Amen.

Share your thoughts

Eight night:

How do you feel?

....
....
....
....
....
....
....
....
....
....
....
....
....
....

What has the word of God taught you?

....
....
....
....
....
....
....
....
....
....
....
....
....
....

How are yours and your baby's sleeping hours?

....
....
....
....
....
....
....
....
....
....
....
....
....
....

Elrich Martin

Is there any improvement and what have you learned?

....
....
....
....
....
....
....
....
....
....
....
....
....
....

DAY NINE

Jeremiah 30:6

"Ask now, and see, can a man bear a child? Why then do I see every man with his hands on his stomach like a woman in labor? Why has every face turned pale?"

This verse says it all. No man can even think off filling the duties of a mother, a woman, a wife. No man will survive the test of pregnancy of labor, I as a man can confess. That is why God made man and then woman as God knew that the real duty can only be done with the heart of a woman. The above verse references to the strength of a woman. Even after the pain of first labor, woman still has the courage to go for the second one and the third and you know Even the strongest man in the world will not be able to fill the shoes of the smallest mother. You are a strong woman, declare it and receive it, in Jesus name.

Prayer for today:

Lord thank you for giving me the privilege to be a woman, to be a mother and a wife. I feel so impatient with this. I think the tiredness is taking over. Please, Lord, renew my mind and give me the strength to go on. Amen.

Share your thoughts

Ninth night:

How do you feel?

....
....
....
....
....
....
....
....
....
....
....
....
....

What has the word of God taught you?

....
....
....
....
....

....
....
....
....
....
....
....
....
....

How are yours and your baby's sleeping hours?

....
....
....
....
....
....
....
....
....
....
....
....
....
....

Is there any improvement and what have you learned?

....
....

Elrich Martin

....
....
....
....
....
....
....
....
....
....
....
....

DAY TEN

Genesis 3:20

"The man called his wife's name Eve because she was the mother of all living."

Woman, you spiritual names are all Eve as you are the mother of all living; the honor of being able to multiply through you and bear a living testimony within you. Mary carried the great I AM within her womb, the son of God. Be at peace that you are looking after a living testimony and as they suckle on you, they are feeding of your strengths and will one day be called to greatness and you can claim the motherly status of a future pastor, worship singer, evangelist, bishop, you name it. Visualize their destiny as you look after them and see how God will manifest their future through your belief.

Prayer for today:

Lord, it looks like my little one is sleeping an hour longer tonight than normal and I thank you for this progress. It gives me more to be grateful for and I love you, my Father. Amen.

Share your thoughts

Tenth night:

How do you feel?

....
....
....
....
....
....
....
....
....
....
....
....
....
....

What has the word of God taught you?

....
....
....
....
....
....
....
....

....
....
....
....
....
....

How are yours and your baby's sleeping hours?

....
....
....
....
....
....
....
....
....
....
....
....
....
....

Is there any improvement and what have you learned?

....
....
....
....
....

Elrich Martin

....
....
....
....
....
....
....
....
....

DAY ELEVEN

Jeremiah 31:25

"I will refresh the weary and satisfy the faint."

The word of God will refresh your spirit and mind. You will be refreshed and have renewed energy. You will not feel weary or feel depressed. You are a warrior woman and a mighty mother of faith.

Prayer for today:

Lord, I'm happy for the word you gave me today. Please renew my strength. Please give me a fresh spirit of hope. In Jesus name I ask, Amen.

Share your thoughts

Eleventh night:

How do you feel?

....

....

43

Elrich Martin

....
....
....
....
....
....
....
....
....
....
....
....

What has the word of God taught you?

....
....
....
....
....
....
....
....
....
....
....

How are yours and your baby's sleeping hours?

....
....
....

....
....
....
....
....
....
....
....
....
....
....

Is there any improvement and what have you learned?

....
....
....
....
....
....
....
....
....
....
....
....
....

DAY TWELVE

Isaiah 40:29

He gives strength to the weary and increases the power of the weak.

You will not grow tired and you will draw strength from the word of God. As you sit, feeling tired and hopeless, stand up brush your hair, look in the mirror and smile and declare you are full of joy, energy and desire to finish the test and give your little one a hug as only a mother can.

Prayer for today:

God, I know everything will be octal is well and I believe it can only get better. I praise your name, Lord. Amen.

Share your thoughts

Twelfth night:

How do you feel?

....
....
....
....
....
....
....
....
....
....
....
....
....
....

What has the word of God taught you?

....
....
....
....
....
....
....
....
....
....
....
....
....
....

Elrich Martin

How are yours and your baby's sleeping hours?

....
....
....
....
....
....
....
....
....
....
....
....
....
....

Is there any improvement and what have you learned?

....
....
....
....
....
....
....
....
....
....
....
....

DAY THIRTEEN

Psalm 4:8

In peace I will lie down and sleep, for you alone, Lord, make me dwell in safety."

Your day of rest is closer than you think, both the inner peace and the utterly rest you crave. Look at your pillow and say, be prepared, I'm coming and my rest is on the way. Even after thirteen days, you are still standing. Be proud of yourself. You are almost there.

Prayer for today:

Father, thank you for giving me peace within the storm. Please calm my heart and mind and help me focus only on you as I do my motherly duties. I ask all in Jesus name, Amen.

Share your thoughts

Thirteenth night:

How do you feel?

Elrich Martin

....
....
....
....
....
....
....
....
....
....
....
....

What has the word of God taught you?

....
....
....
....
....
....
....
....
....
....
....
....
....

How are yours and your baby's sleeping hours?

....
....
....
....
....
....
....
....
....
....
....
....
....

Is there any improvement and what have you learned?

....
....
....
....
....
....
....
....
....
....
....
....
....

DAY FOURTEEN

Romans 8:26-28

In the same way, the Spirit helps us in our weakness. We do not know what we ought to pray for, but the Spirit himself intercedes for us through wordless groans. And he who searches our hearts knows the mind of the Spirit because the Spirit intercedes for God's people in accordance with the will of God. And we know that in all things God works for the good of those who love him, who have been called according to his purpose.

Please meditate on this word as a source of inspiration for your day.

Prayer for today:

Lord, give me the strength with my weakness and joy in my heart to go on as I feel weary. I thank you for your supernatural strength. Amen.

Share your thoughts

Fourteenth night:

How do you feel?

....
....
....
....
....
....
....
....
....
....
....
....
....

What has the word of God taught you?

....
....
....
....
....
....
....
....
....
....
....
....

Elrich Martin

....
....

How are yours and your baby's sleeping hours?

....
....
....
....
....
....
....
....
....
....
....
....
....
....

Is there any improvement and what have you learned?

....
....
....
....
....
....
....
....
....
....

....
....
....

DAY FIFTEEN

Psalm 73:26

My flesh and my heart may fail, but God is the strength of my heart and my portion forever.

As human beings, we all fail sometimes in our efforts, even mothers. If your heart feels troubled by worries for your baby, look to God and thank him for his grace upon your life so you can be a light in your little one life. Ask God to take out your stony heart and put in a hurt of flesh so you can renew your heart and jumpstart your purpose in the Lord for your child. What God started in your life he will finish and you will receive your reward.

Prayer for today:

God, please give me the will to go on and make me a better person as I feel weak in faith. Please restore my faith and help me to look on the finished work on the cross. Amen.

Share your thoughts

Fifteenth night:

How do you feel?

....
....
....
....
....
....
....
....
....
....
....
....
....

What has the word of God taught you?

....
....
....
....
....
....
....
....

....
....
....
....

How are yours and your baby's sleeping hours?

....
....
....
....
....
....
....
....
....
....
....
....
....
....

Is there any improvement and what have you learned?

....
....
....
....
....
....
....
....
....
....

Elrich Martin

....

....

....

DAY SIXTEEN

Proverbs 3:24

When you lie down, you will not be afraid; when you lie down, your sleep will be sweet."

Don't these words sound like heaven? Hmmm, sleep and more sleep. When you give your cares over to God, your rest will be sweet, your worries will be no more and you will not fear. You have a little angel in your arms and soon both of you will lay in sweet calmeth of God's grace. Your time is almost there, receive it.

Prayer for today:

Thank you, Lord, for giving me rest and to fill me with calmeth. Guide me, teach me, and restore me In Jesus name I ask, Amen.

Share your thoughts

Sixteenth night:

How do you feel?

Elrich Martin

....
....
....
....
....
....
....
....
....
....
....
....
....
....

What has the word of God taught you?

....
....
....
....
....
....
....
....
....
....
....
....
....

How are yours and your baby's sleeping hours?

....
....
....
....
....
....
....
....
....
....
....
....
....
....

Is there any improvement and what have you learned?

....
....
....
....
....
....
....
....
....
....
....
....
....

DAY SEVENTEEN

Exodus 33:14

The Lord replied, "My Presence will go with you, and I will give you rest."

God will give you rest, spiritual, emotional and spiritual. You can probably image it now and are actually feeling the sleep within calling. Be of good cheer, these word within the bible is just for you.

Prayer for today:

Lord thank you for your presence in my life and thank you for rest in abundance. Thank you for your guidance and bringing calmeth to my mind. Amen.

Share your thoughts

Seventeenth night:

How do you feel?

....
....
....
....
....
....
....
....
....
....
....
....
....

What has the word of God taught you?

....
....
....
....
....
....
....
....
....
....
....
....
....
....

How are yours and your baby's sleeping hours?

....
....
....
....
....
....
....
....
....
....
....
....
....
....

Is there any improvement and what have you learned?

....
....
....
....
....
....
....
....
....
....
....

The Praying Mommy

....
....

DAY EIGHTEEN

Psalm 46:10

"Be still, and know that I am God. I will be exalted among the nations; I will be exalted in the earth!"

In times of distress, be still and expect the good things God have for you. It doesn't have to be quiet around for you to be still within. It's with the chaos surrounding us that stillness within us will be most effective in being victorious. Be still and believe.

Prayer for today:

Father, help me to be still and only hear your voice as I take on the night with hope and joy. You are the alpha and omega of our faith. Thank you for your love. In Jesus name, Amen.

Share your thoughts

Eighteenth night:

How do you feel?

....
....
....
....
....
....
....
....
....
....
....
....
....
....

What has the word of God taught you?

....
....
....
....
....
....
....
....
....
....
....
....
....

Elrich Martin

How are yours and your baby's sleeping hours?

....
....
....
....
....
....
....
....
....
....
....
....
....
....

Is there any improvement and what have you learned?

....
....
....
....
....
....
....
....
....
....
....
....
....

DAY NINETEEN

Philippians 4:13

"I can do all things through him who strengthens me."

By now I believe you are full of the energy and expectation of Gods rest for you and his strength with your weakness. Worship if you feel like it, shout out to God. This is a new day and things can only get better.

Prayer for today:

My strength lies in you Lord. Please guides my steps and renew my thoughts. In Jesus name I ask, Amen.

<u>Share your thoughts</u>

Nineteenth night:

How do you feel?

....

....

....

Elrich Martin

....
....
....
....
....
....
....
....
....
....
....

What has the word of God taught you?

....
....
....
....
....
....
....
....
....
....
....
....
....

How are yours and your baby's sleeping hours?

....
....
....
....
....
....
....
....
....
....
....
....
....
....

Is there any improvement and what have you learned?

....
....
....
....
....
....
....
....
....
....
....
....
....
....

DAY TWENTY

Isaiah 30:15

"...In quietness and trust is your strength ..."

You are most at the end point and you have learnt to be quiet and trust in the lord, knowing that the struggle is almost over. Keep your eyes fixed on Jesus and your faith in his strength through you.

Prayer for today:

God, I am almost there, the storm is almost over and I thank you. You are a rock and my strength. Amen.

Share your thoughts

Twentieth night:

How do you feel?

....

....

....

....
....
....
....
....
....
....
....
....
....
....

What has the word of God taught you?

....
....
....
....
....
....
....
....
....
....
....

How are yours and your baby's sleeping hours?

....
....
....

Elrich Martin

....
....
....
....
....
....
....
....
....
....
....

Is there any improvement and what have you learned?

....
....
....
....
....
....
....
....
....
....
....
....
....
....

DAY TWENTY-ONE

Isaiah 40:11

"He tends his flock like a shepherd; he will gather the lambs in his arms, he will carry them in his bosom, and gently lead those that are with young."

This is Gods direct promise to you. He promises to guide you through the struggles and he know the issues with having young, therefore God is leading you, holding your hand and leading you forward, day by day till you reached your destination.

Prayer for today:

Thank you, Father, for your promise you have for me and that you are leading my way. Thank you for the love you have for me. Amen

Share your thoughts

Twenty-first night:

How do you feel?

75

Elrich Martin

....
....
....
....
....
....
....
....
....
....
....
....
....
....

What has the word of God taught you?

....
....
....
....
....
....
....
....
....
....
....
....
....
....

How are yours and your baby's sleeping hours?

....
....
....
....
....
....
....
....
....
....
....
....
....

Is there any improvement and what have you learned?

....
....
....
....
....
....
....
....
....
....
....
....
....

DAY TWENTY-TWO

Isaiah 54:5

"For your Maker is your husband, the Lord of hosts is his name, and the Holy One of Israel is your Redeemer; the God of the whole earth he is called."

For all the single mothers and mothers that do not have present husbands in their test, be a peace that God have taken over the duty of your husband and he will never leave you, nor forsake you. He will always listen to the desires of your heart and he will never condemn you. He loves you and he is your provider.

Prayer for today:

Father, you are my husband and my provider. You know my heart and mind. You are my fortress and my rock. Thank you for saving me. Amen.

Share your thoughts

Twenty-second night:

How do you feel?

....
....
....
....
....
....
....
....
....
....
....
....
....
....

What has the word of God taught you?

....
....
....
....
....
....
....
....
....
....
....
....
....
....

Elrich Martin

How are yours and your baby's sleeping hours?

....
....
....
....
....
....
....
....
....
....
....
....
....
....
.....

Is there any improvement and what have you learned?

....
....
....
....
....
....
....
....
....
....
....
....
....

DAY TWENTY-THREE

Psalm 105:4

"Seek the LORD and his strength; seek his presence continually!"

Always seek God first in your storm. Look to God for answers every time, all the time and he will give you the answers you seek.

Prayer for today:

Father, I keep my eyes focused on you and only you. My joy is from you and no one else. Amen.

Share your thoughts

Twenty-third night:

How do you feel?

....
....
....

Elrich Martin

....
....
....
....
....
....
....
....
....
....
....

What has the word of God taught you?

....
....
....
....
....
....
....
....
....
....
....
....
....

How are yours and your baby's sleeping hours?

....
....

....
....
....
....
....
....
....
....
....
....
....

Is there any improvement and what have you learned?

....
....
....
....
....
....
....
....
....
....
....
....
....
....

DAY TWENTY-FOUR

Nehemiah 8:10

"...the joy of the LORD is your strength."

Be happy, jump up and down if you like and rejoice and praise God for your victory. You are closer to rest then you think.

Prayer for today:

Thank you for joy within my test, for strength within weakness or calmeth within the turmoil.

Amen.

<u>Share your thoughts</u>

Twenty-fourth night:

How do you feel?

....
....
....

....
....
....
....
....
....
....
....
....
....
....

What has the word of God taught you?

....
....
....
....
....
....
....
....
....
....
....
....

How are yours and your baby's sleeping hours?

....
....
....

Elrich Martin

....
....
....
....
....
....
....
....
....
....
....

Is there any improvement and what have you learned?

....
....
....
....
....
....
....
....
....
....
....
....
....
....

DAY TWENTY-FIVE

Psalm 118:5

"Out of my distress I called on the Lord; the Lord answered me and set me free."

Your prayers are being answered. You can feel the expectation of victory within your spirit as if you are about to win the ultimate prize. God heard your hearts cry. He loves you and only wants the best for you.

Prayer for today:

Thank you, God, for hearing my prayer and drying my tears and giving me hope. Amen.

Share your thoughts

Twenty-fifth night:

How do you feel?

....

....

Elrich Martin

....
....
....
....
....
....
....
....
....
....
....
....

What has the word of God taught you?

....
....
....
....
....
....
....
....
....
....
....
....

How are yours and your baby's sleeping hours?

....
....

....
....
....
....
....
....
....
....
....
....
....

Is there any improvement and what have you learned?

....
....
....
....
....
....
....
....
....
....
....
....
....

DAY TWENTY-SIX

Psalm 34:18

"The Lord is close to the brokenhearted and saves those who are crushed in spirit."

Let the words for God be a soothing feeling to your mind and spirit knowing that the test always seems worse just before the end of the line but God is healing your broken spirit.

Prayer for today:

Thank you for mending my spirit and heart father and giving me fresh hope for a new day. Amen.

Share your thoughts

Twenty-sixth night:

How do you feel?

....

....

....
....
....
....
....
....
....
....
....
....
....
....

What has the word of God taught you?

....
....
....
....
....
....
....
....
....
....
....

How are yours and your baby's sleeping hours?

....
....

Elrich Martin

....
....
....
....
....
....
....
....
....
....
....
....

Is there any improvement and what have you learned?

....
....
....
....
....
....
....
....
....
....
....
....
....
....

DAY TWENTY-SEVEN

Philemon 1:20

"...Refresh my heart in Christ."

Refresh your tired heart in Christ and you will be victorious.

Prayer for today:

Father, I thank you of the renewing of my heart and for giving me hope. Amen.

Share your thoughts

Twenty-seventh night:

How do you feel?

....

....

....

....

....

Elrich Martin

....
....
....
....
....
....
....
....
....

What has the word of God taught you?

....
....
....
....
....
....
....
....
....
....
....
....
....

How are yours and your baby's sleeping hours?

....
....
....
....

....
....
....
....
....
....
....
....
....
....

Is there any improvement and what have you learned?

....
....
....
....
....
....
....
....
....
....
....
....
....
....

DAY TWENTY-EIGHT

Isaiah 40:31

"But those who wait on the LORD shall renew their strength; they shall mount up with wings like eagles, they shall run and not be weary, they shall walk and not faint.

Let this word of God be a source of strength and a testimony of what God will do for and through you.

Prayer for today:

Thank you, father, for your word in Isaiah 40:31 that show you shall renew my strength if I wait for you. Thank you for a refreshed mind. Amen.

Share your thoughts

Twenty-eight night:

How do you feel?

....

....

....
....
....
....
....
....
....
....
....
....
....
....

What has the word of God taught you?

....
....
....
....
....
....
....
....
....
....
....
....

How are yours and your baby's sleeping hours?

....
....

Elrich Martin

....
....
....
....
....
....
....
....
....
....
....
....

Is there any improvement and what have you
learned?

....
....
....
....
....
....
....
....
....
....
....
....
....

DAY TWENTY-NINE

Romans 12:12

"Rejoice in hope, be patient in tribulation, be constant in prayer."

You can't contain yourself at this time. God have laid the seeds of joy and hope within your heart. Your patience is a sign of the faith you have obtained through prayer as you wait.

Prayer for today:

Thank you, father, for teaching me patience, faith and joy through your world and showing me how it applies it when faced with a storm. Amen.

Share your thoughts

Twenty-ninth night:

How do you feel?

Elrich Martin

....
....
....
....
....
....
....
....
....
....
....
....
....
....

What has the word of God taught you?

....
....
....
....
....
....
....
....
....
....
....
....
....
....

How are yours and your baby's sleeping hours?

....
....
....
....
....
....
....
....
....
....
....
....
....
....

Is there any improvement and what have you learned?

....
....
....
....
....
....
....
....
....
....
....
....

Elrich Martin

....

....

DAY THIRTY

Psalm 43:5

"Why are you cast down, O my soul, and why are you in turmoil within me? Hope in God; for I shall again praise him, my salvation and my God."

Don't let your emoting rob you of what God have in store for you. Worship and praise and believe in God who loves you more than you know. Lay your head on His chest as you receive his peace.

Prayer for today:

Father, the enemy tried to attack my mind today but I resisted the Devil and place my hope and faith in you my Lord. I praise you with all my heart. Amen.

Share your thoughts

Thirtieth night:

How do you feel?

Elrich Martin

....
....
....
....
....
....
....
....
....
....
....
....
....
....

What has the word of God taught you?

....
....
....
....
....
....
....
....
....
....
....
....
....
....

How are yours and your baby's sleeping hours?

....
....
....
....
....
....
....
....
....
....
....
....
....

Is there any improvement and what have you learned?

....
....
....
....
....
....
....
....
....
....
....
....

DAY THIRTY-ONE

2 Corinthians 12:9

"But he said to me' "My grace is sufficient for you, for my power is made perfect in weakness." Therefore I will boast all the more gladly of my weaknesses so that the power of Christ may rest upon me."

For thirty days you have learnt how to stay strong in faith during the night shift of looking after your little one. I believe God have held you in the palm of his hand during this time and that your little one is now giving you the rest you need. Mothers, we as men salute you for your sacrifice to raise four children through the word of God and we appreciate you more than you know. God is smiling down on you, knowing that you were his ultimate creation of trust and love. You are loved and you are highly favored. Be of good cheer, mommy, all is well.

Prayer for today:

Thank you, father, for your grace during this time of endorsement and things can only get better. My heart feels renewed, my mind feel and ease and my spirit feels at rest. Thank you for your word and the promises you have in our time of test. I love you, Father. Amen.

Share your thoughts

Thirty-first night:

How do you feel?

....
....
....
....
....
....
....
....
....
....
....

What has the word of God taught you?

....
....
....
....
....
....
....
....
....
....
....
....

Elrich Martin

How are yours and baby's sleeping hours?

....
....
....
....
....
....
....
....
....
....
....
....
....

Is there any improvement and what have you learned?

....
....
....
....
....
....
....
....
....
....
....
....
....
....

Elrich Martin

CPSIA information can be obtained
at www.ICGtesting.com
Printed in the USA
LVOW10s0635180917
549068LV00022BA/638/P